ISBN 978-0-260-54720-0
PIBN 10955371

rchive Document

ontent reflects current scientific knowledge,
ces.

$\overset{2}{\overset{Pa}{}}$

THE Demand and Price SITUATION

BUREAU OF AGRICULTURAL ECONOMICS
UNITED STATES DEPARTMENT OF AGRICULTURE

WASHINGTON D C.   BAE   SEPTEMBER 1948

Approved by the Outlook and Situation Board, October 4, 1948

SUMMARY

A strong demand for most farm products is expected in 1949. If economic trends and government programs develop in accordance with current indications, prices to be received by farmers and cash receipts from farm marketings in 1949 may average almost as high as in 1948. However, farm production costs are expected to remain high and net incomes to farm operators are likely to be less than in 1948.

Present forces indicate, in total, a fairly stable level of economic activity in 1949. Substantial amounts of foreign aid and the growing rate of Government expenditures for defense afford considerable assurance for a high level of demand, at least for the first half of next year. There is even a possibility that the impact of these expenditures on a generally tight economy may cause some further price inflation. But any further price advances are likely to be principally in nonagricultural commodities.

Demand prospects are more uncertain for the second half of 1949 when crop and livestock marketings will be heavy. The major uncertainty pertains to the size of next year's expenditures for the national defense and foreign aid. Although recent developments have tightened the international situation, it is conceivable that they could change in such a way as to result in substantial cutbacks in these programs. This could cause an appreciable weakening of the demand for farm products. But even under such a situation, it is unlikely that cash receipts from farm marketings for the year as a whole would be more than 10 percent below the 30 billion dollars estimated for 1948.

This uncertainty aside, however, no marked reduction in consumer incomes and the domestic demand for farm products generally, can be foreseen for the immediate future. In addition to the probable continued growth in federal government expenditures for defense and related programs, state and local government expenditures for construction of schools, streets and highways are also expanding rapidly and are likely to remain high next year. Shortages of several major consumer goods, notably automobiles and housing, still exist despite high level output in recent years. However, some easing in certain areas appears likely. Deferred demands have been largely met in textiles, shoes and some durable goods. Also, the exceptionally high rate of business expenditures for new plant and equipment in recent years indicates a strong possibility for reduced outlays beginning sometime in 1949.

ECONOMIC TRENDS AFFECTING AGRICULTURE

Item	Unit or base Period	1947 Year	1947 August	1948 May	1948 June	1948 July	1948 August
Industrial production 1/	1935-39						
Total......................	=100	187	182	192	192	186	190
All manufacturers.........	do.	194	188	197	198	191	196
Durable goods.............	do.	220	210	221	222	219	221
Nondurable goods..........	do.	172	169	178	179	169	176
Minerals...................	do.	149	150	162	159	153	159
Construction activity 1/	1935-39						
Contracts, total............	=100	274	289	328	350	357	
Contracts, residential......	do.	348	368	404	434	458	
Wholesale prices 2/	1926=100						
All commodities.............		152	154	164	166	169	169
All commodities except farm and food........	do.	135	136	149	150	151	153
Farm products.............	do.	181	182	189	196	195	191,
Food......................	do.	169	172	177	181	188	190
Prices received and paid by farmers 3/	1910-14 =100						
Prices received, all prod...	do.	278	276	289	295	301	293
Prices paid, int. & taxes...	do.	231	234	250	251	251	251
Parity ratio...............	do.	120	118	116	118	120	117
Consumers' price 5/ 6/	1935-39						
Total.....................	=100	159	160	170	172	174	174
Food......................	do.	194	196	211	214	217	217
Nonfood...................	do.	140	140	148	148	150	
Income							
Nonagricultural payments 4/	Bil.dol.	174.9	173.1	184.4	187.7	188.2	
Income of industrial workers 3/...............	1935-39 =100	332	333	349	360	361	
Factory payrolls 5/...........	do.	353	353	369	382	383	
Weekly earnings of factory workers 5/							
All manufacturing..........	Dollars	49.26	49.17	51.76	52.95	53.08	53.86
Durable goods.............	do.	52.47	52.46	54.65	56.32	56.46	57.83
Nondurable goods..........	do.	45.87	45.78	48.61	49.39	49.50	49.77
Employment							
Total civilian 7/...........	Millions	58.0	59.6	58.7	61.3	61.6	61.2
Nonagricultural 7/........	do.	49.8	50.6	50.8	51.9	52.5	52.8
Agricultural 7/...........	do.	8.3	9.0	7.9	9.4	9.2	8.4
Government finance (Fed.) 8/							
Income, cash operating......	Mil.dol.	3,909	3,212	3,334	5,105	2,404	
Outgo, cash operating......	do.	3,431	3,173	2,871	4,340	2,765	
Net cash opr.income or outgo	do.	+478	+ 41	+462	+765	-361	

Annual data for the years 1929-47 appear on page 17 of the March 1948 issue of the D
and Price Situation. Sources: 1/ Federal Reserve Board, converted to 1935-39 base.
2/ U. S. Dept. of Labor, BLS. 3/ U. S. Dept. of Agriculture, BAE, to convert prices
ceived and prices paid, interest and taxes, to the 1935-39 base, multiply by .93110
.78125 respectively. 4/ U. S. Dept. of Commerce revised figures employing new conce
seasonally adjusted at annual rate. 5/ U. S. Dept. of Labor, BLS. 6/ Consumers' pr
index for moderate-income families in large cities. 7/ U. S. Dept. of Commerce, Bur
of the Census. 8/ U. S. Dept. of Treasury. Data for 1947 are on average monthly ba

If the European recovery program is extended in line with the size
of the program originally discussed, the volume of U. S. agricultural
exports in 1949 is not likely to be appreciably different than in 1948.
Foreign requirements remain large despite marked improvement in European
crop production this year. Even if further improvement should occur in
1949, some easing in shipments of food grains probably would be offset by
increased shipments of cotton and tobacco, and of feed grains to rebuild
livestock numbers. Moreover, foreign needs for the most part are for
crops for which supplies are more than adequate for domestic needs.

On the basis of continued high levels of consumer income and with
agricultural exports close to 1948 levels, the general level of prices received by farmers in 1949 would be near that of 1948. Under the impact
of 1948 record crop production, a considerable decline in crop prices
has occurred. Prices of many major crops have fallen to or are approaching
support levels. However, the general level of agricultural prices has been
relatively well maintained by advancing prices for livestock and livestock
products, which are in shorter supply in 1948 than a year ago.

Even if crop production in 1949 is heavy, only minor declines in
prices of the basic crops (corn, wheat, cotton, tobacco, rice and peanuts)
could occur under existing price support legislation. Support levels for
these 1949 crops may be slightly below 1948 levels as a result of lower
prices for feed and some other commodities purchased by farmers. Support
levels for other crops, such as potatoes and flaxseed, could be set at
lower levels than in 1948 under existing legislation. The record 1948
feed crops will be reflected in increases in supplies of livestock and
livestock products with lower prices likely in the second half of 1949.
Moreover, expanding livestock operations would increase the outlets for feed
grains.

Even though crop production next year is likely to be somewhat below
the 1948 record, increasing livestock output may maintain the total volume
of farm marketings at about the 1948 level. Total cash receipts from farm
marketings may be down slightly, primarily because of lower prices in
the second half of the year. Realized net income of farm operators is also
likely to be lower in 1949 as production costs are expected to remain as
high as in 1948. Although feed costs probably will be down, other
important expenses such as labor costs, depreciation charges, interest
and tax payments, and motor-vehicle operating costs are likely to increase.

Commodity highlights

Strong consumer demand is expected to maintain prices of meat animals
in 1949 close to the 1948 level, but sharply increased hog marketings expected late in 1949 probably will cause pork prices to drop more than
seasonally. Demand for milk and dairy products will also continue at high
levels, with prices averaging about the same as this year. Prices of eggs
are likely to average almost as high in 1949 as in 1948 but prices of
chickens, broilers and turkeys probably will average lower next year, with
most of the decrease during the latter months of the year. The general
level of fat-and-oil prices is likely to be moderately lower during the
season just beginning than in the previous season, largely as a result of
increased domestic production.

Chiefly as a result of the large production, feed prices are expected to average much lower in 1948-49 than in the past feeding season. Prices of all feed grains are expected to be close to the Government support levels this fall and winter and to be unusually low relative to livestock prices. Wheat prices are also likely to be close to support levels, with another increase in stocks. Consumer demand for fruit in 1949 probably will be about the same as in 1948. However, if production next year is larger than this year's below average crop, prices will be somewhat lower. Sugar supplies in the U. S. are expected to be ample next year. As authorized by the Agricultural Act of 1948, the level of price-support for 1949-crop potatoes will probably be set lower than the 90 percent of parity which applies to the 1948 crop. Demand for truck crops through most of 1949 is expected to be about as strong as in 1948. Prices received by farmers for fresh market truck crops probably will average lower because production is likely to be larger. Demand for dry edible beans in 1949 probably will be moderately lower than in 1948, mainly because of an expected reduction in export demand.

While domestic demand for cotton will probably be weaker this season than in the previous one, exports as likely to be larger than the very low level in the 1947-48 season. World demand for wool is expected to continue strong. Consumer demand for cigarettes during 1949 will continue high and export demand for unmanufactured tobacco will be stronger. Demand, and also prices, for forest products are expected to continue generally strong, although some decline from the high level in 1948 is likely.

THE DEMAND FOR FARM PRODUCTS IN 1948

Exceptionally high demand for food and other farm products in recent years has stemmed from record consumer incomes generated by the postwar boom and by extremely large foreign needs. For three years, employment and wages, production and prices have been increasing. In 1948, they combined to produce the highest consumer incomes and the highest value of output (gross national product) in history. As indicated in table 1, the gross national product in 1948 was 3 times as large as in 1935-39, with increased physical output (including agricultural) and higher prices contributing almost equally to this tremendous advance. During the past year, however, the 8 percent increase in value of the national output was primarily due to rising prices, reflecting the inflationary forces in the economy.

DOMESTIC DEMAND IN 1948

Employment

During 1947 and 1948, the domestic economy has had practically full employment. In the past year, a moderate increase in the civilian labor force has been absorbed without difficulty. In August 1948, total civilian employment was more than 61 million persons, almost a million and a half over August 1947 and 15 million more than in 1939. Unemployment in August 1948 was slightly below 2 million and has not been far from that level during most of the postwar boom. Unemployment of 2 million is considered to be close to a minimum. For the most part, it is made up of persons moving from one job to another.

Table 1.- Selected series of production, prices, employment and income,
1935-39 average, and 1946-1948.

Item	Base period or unit	Calendar year		
		1935-39 average	1946	1947	1948 Est.
)tal civilian employment 1/	Million	44.6	55.2	58.0	59.4
1employment 1/	Do.	9.4	2.3	2.1	1.8
ndustrial production 2/	1935-39	100	170	187	192
Durable goods	Do.	100	192	220	225
Nondurable goods	Do.	100	165	172	176
onsumers' prices (urban) 3/	Do.	100	139.3	159.2	172
Food	Do.	100	159.6	193.8	210
Nonfood	Do.	100	128.0	139.7	149
Wholesale prices, all commodities 3/	1926	81	121.1	152.1	167
Farm products	Do.	76	148.9	181.2	190
Food products	Do.	79	130.7	168.7	178
All exol. farm and food	Do.	81	109.5	135.2	150
Prices received by farmers	Aug. 1909-July 1914	107	233	278	291
Prices paid, int. & taxes	1910-14	128	193	231	250
Parity price ratio		84	121	120	116
Farm cash income, including Government payments	Bil. dol.	8.5	25.6	30.5	30.2
Realized net income of farm operators	Do.	4.3	15.0	17.9	16.5
Volume of farm marketings	1935-39	100	139	143	140
Gross national product 4/	Bil. dol.	84.0	209.3	231.6	251
Personal consumption expd.	Do.	63.6	147.4	164.8	177
Gross private domestic investment	Bil. dol.	8.2	26.5	30.0	38
New construction	Do.	3.1	8.9	11.7	15
Producers' durable eqpt.	Do.	4.4	12.8	17.8	20
Change in business inventories	Do.	1.2	4.8	.6	3
Net foreign investment	Do.	.4	4.7	8.9	4
Government purchases of goods and services	Do.	11.8	30.8	28.0	32
Personal income 4/	Do.	67.2	178.1	195.2	209
Disposable personal income 4/	Do.	66.2	159.2	173.6	189

1/ Bureau of the Census and BLS. 2/ Federal Reserve Board. 3/ Bureau of Labor Statistics. 4/ United States Department of Commerce.

All of the increase in employment since prewar has occurred off the
farm. Agricultural employment is more than a million smaller than before
the war.

Compared with 1939, the number of wage and salary workers in manufacturing has increased about 6 million, with most of the gain in the
durable goods industries. Other increases were: trade, 3 million;
services, 1.5 million; federal, state and local governments, 1.5 million;
construction, 1 million; transportation and public utilities, 1 million.
Increases in mining and finance were smaller.

Industrial Production

Industrial production also has been maintained at a high, stable level
during 1948. In August, the Federal Reserve Board index of industrial production was 191 (1935-39=100) and is likely to average close to that figure
for the year as a whole. This would be slightly above the average of 187
in 1947. While the current level of total production is considerably below
the war years when armament production was heavily weighted in the index, it
is close to peak output in view of some material shortages. Compared with
1947, all three of the major components in the index (durable and non-
durable manufactures and minerals) showed minor gains.

Production in the durable goods group, which reflects output in such
industries as steel, machinery and building materials, has more than doubled
since prewar. In some fields, notably steel and automobiles, production
has not been sufficient to meet the heavy demands resulting from wartime
restrictions on the production of civilian goods. The non-durable goods
industries, which were relatively well maintained during the war, have been
producing about three-fourths more than before the war. Deferred demands
for this group of commodities have largely been met. Recently, production
of textiles and shoes has been trending downward. Mineral production
(mainly coal and oil) has been relatively stable at about 60 percent above
prewar.

Commodity Prices

The General Price Level. Despite the record peacetime production during
the past three years, the unprecedented domestic and foreign demand for
most commodities has been great enough to cause prices to advance through
most of the period. In the summer of 1948, the general price level was
the highest on record. The Bureau of Labor Statistics all-commodity index
of wholesale prices in August 1948 was 169 (1926=100), 10 percent above
August 1947 and slightly above the post World War I peak of 167 reached in
May 1920. Since June 1946, when many price controls were ended, this
index has advanced about 50 percent.

The rise in prices last spring after the abrupt decline in February of
some commodities, largely agricultural, reflected "third-round" wage increases,
the reduction in income taxes and to some extent the outlook for larger
expenditures for defense and foreign aid. In early September, there were
indications that the major price adjustments to these factors had occurred.

Table 2.-Group indexes of wholesale prices, August 1947 and 1948
(1926=100)

Commodity group	August 1948	August 1947	Percent change from August 1947
Fuel and lighting materials	137	113	+ 21
Metals and metal products	171	148	+ 16
Building materials	203	180	+ 13
Chemical and allied products	132	118	+ 12
House furnishings	145	130	+ 12
Foods	190	172	+ 10
Farm products	191	182	+ 5
Textile products	148	142	+ 4
Hides and leather products	188	183	+ 3
All other than farm and food	153	136	+ 12
All commodities	169	154	+ 10

As shown in table 2, price increases have been greatest during the past year in fuels and lighting materials, metals and metal products and building materials. On the other hand, price advances in textile products, hides and leather products have been relatively small.

Agricultural Prices. Agricultural prices are among those showing relatively small increases over a year ago. The record crop production this year, which is expected to total about 9 percent above the previous record in 1946, has been reflected in declining crop prices. Since January, when these prices were generally at record levels, prices received by farmers for crops have declined an average of 19 percent. During January-September, prices of food grains declined 31 percent, feed grains and hay 30 percent, oil bearing crops 25 percent and cotton 6 percent. However, the general level of prices received by farmers in September was only 6 percent below January, as prices of livestock and livestock products have advanced 5 percent. Similar offsets are shown in the comparison with September a year ago.

Compared with September 1947, prices received for crops were down 9 percent, with all groups, except tobacco and fruits, showing declines. However, prices of the livestock groups averaged 9 percent higher and the overall level was slightly above September 1947. Since prices of many of the major farm crops are at or approaching support levels, further downward price adjustments in the general level on the basis of the current crops are likely to be small. Supplies of livestock and its products are smaller this year than last, primarily because of the small 1947 corn crop, and demand continues exceptionally strong.

Prices Paid by Farmers. The overall level of prices paid by farmers for commodities, interest and taxes has been relatively stable during recent months. Rising prices for most items used in living and in production have been offset by sharp declines in food prices. From August to September, this index declined 1 point to 250 (1910-14=100), and was 5 percent higher than in September 1947. The parity ratio in September--the ratio of prices received by farmers to prices paid for commodities, and taxes--was 116, compared with 120 a year ago and 84 in 1935-39.

Table 3.-Group indexes of prices received by farmers, September 1947 and 1948
(1909-14=100)

Group	September 1948	September 1947	Percent change from Sept. 1947
Feed grains and hay	223	297	- 25
Food grains	223	278	- 20
Truck crops	150	179	- 16
Oil bearing crops	282	311	- 9
Cotton	250	252	- 1
Fruits	185	181	+ 2
Tobacco	406	352	+ 15
All crops	231	254	- 9
Meat animals	408	367	+ 11
Dairy products	302	282	+ 7
Poultry and eggs	253	246	+ 3
All livestock and products	343	315	+ 9
Crops and livestock	290	286	+ 1

Urban Consumer Prices. The urban retail price level, as measured by the BLS index of consumer prices, continued to move up in August to 175 (1935-39=100) from 174 in July. This represents a rise of 9 percent over August 1947. In the past year, retail food prices have increased 10 percent and non-food items 8 percent.

Wage Rates. Factory wage rates generally have kept pace with the consumer price level in the past year. From July 1947 to July 1948, average hourly earnings in manufacturing rose from $1.23 to $1.33, a gain of 8 percent. A larger gain occurred in the building trades, but the increase in average hourly earnings in retail trade was relatively small. So far this year, there has been little change in the average hours worked per week.

Farm wage rates also continue on an uptrend. In the summer of 1948, they were 7 percent above last summer.

Gross National Product. The major forces contributing to the current boom are indicated in the breakdown of the gross national product (table 1), which measures the total national output at prevailing market prices.

1. Most important has been the tremendous demand for all types of goods and services. This has been due to high employment and steadily advancing wage rates, deferred demands from the war years and the largest individual holdings of liquid assets in history.

During 1946 and 1947, consumer expenditures increased more than consumer incomes. This was possible partly through the use of past savings, a reduction in the rate of saving from current income and through a sharp increase in consumer credit. In 1948, the increase in consumer expenditures has been more moderate than in the previous 2 years and has been less than the increase in consumer incomes. This tendency toward a more normal spending pattern indicates that, in the aggregate, supplies are overtaking demands at current prices. Nevertheless, backlogs of demand for automobiles and housing are still large. While the proportion of consumer incomes going for food increased during 1946 and 1947, it has been quite stable during 1948.

2. The marked expansion in private domestic investment was another important factor. In 1948, these expenditures were almost 5 times prewar. The boom in residential building is likely to set a record in 1948 of almost 1 million new dwelling units started compared with 850,000 in 1947 and 937,000 in the previous record year of 1925. In recent months, however, the volume of new starts has trended downward.

Business capital outlays for plant and equipment have continued at exceptionally high levels in 1948, and further substantial gains were made in modernizing and equipping the nation's industrial plant. In the last two years, expenditures for new equipment have made up a large share of the total gross national product than ever before. Business inventories also continued to expand in 1948.

3. The large excess of United States exports over imports has also been an important factor in the general domestic demand picture (foreign demand for farm products is discussed in a following section). The net foreign investment component of the gross national product in table 1 represents only that part of the export surplus which was not financed by U. S. Government grants. The latter expenditures are shown under the Government component. A more accurate appraisal of current trends in U. S. foreign trade can be obtained from table 4.

U. S. exports and the export surplus (excess of exports over imports) have trended downward since the second quarter of 1947. This has largely reflected dollar shortages in foreign countries. In the second quarter of 1948, the annual rate of U. S. exports was 17 billion dollars, compared with 19.8 billions in 1947 as a whole. The export surplus was reduced to 7 billion dollars compared with 11.3 billions last year. Compared with 1947 the significant changes in the first part of 1948 have been a moderate increase in imports from abroad; a pronounced reduction in dollars obtained from the liquidation of foreign assets; and a large reduction in the second quarter of U. S. Government grants and loans to foreign countries. The latter was due partly to the exhaustion of the British loan, a reduction in the use of interim aid funds and the slow start made in getting ECA underway. However, existing appropriations and expanding expenditures for the several foreign programs, indicate a substantial increase in U. S. exports and the export surplus during the remainder of this year. They may reach the levels of the last half of 1947. It is estimated that 6 billion dollars of U. S. aid will be utilized during 1948. On this basis, U. S. exports of goods and services this year may total about 18.3 billions, only 8 percent below 1947. U. S. imports, during the remainder of 1948, are likely to continue near the levels of the first half of the year.

Table 4.- Financing of United States exports of goods and
services in specified periods.

(Billions of dollars)

Period	U. S. exports of goods and services	U. S. imports of goods and services	Means of financing		
			Sale of gold and short- and long-term dollar assets by foreign countries (Net)	U. S. Govt. grants & loans to foreign countries (Net)	Other sources and balancing Item (Net) 1/
	(1)	(2)	(3)	(4)	(5)
1935-39 ann. average	4.0	3.4	1.1	2/(-) 0.1	(-) 0.4
1946	15.0	7.2	2.0	5.0	0.8
1947					
1st qtr. (ann. rate)	19.3	8.1	4.8	5.2	1.2
2nd qtr. (ann. rate)	21.1	8.6	4.6	7.9	---
3rd qtr. (ann. rate)	19.2	8.3	3.4	6.8	0.7
4th qtr. (ann. rate)	19.4	8.9	5.3	2.9	2.3
Year	19.8	8.5	4.5	5.7	1.1
1948					
1st qtr. (ann. rate)	17.8	10.0	1.2	3/ 5.2	1.4
2nd qtr. (ann. rate)	17.0	10.0	2.8	4/ 3.4	0.8
Est. year				5/ 6.0	

1/ Includes loans of U. S. dollars by the International Bank and by the International Monetary Fund. In 1947 these loans totaled 761 million dollars. In the first half of 1948 they were at the annual rate of 626 million dollars.
2/ Includes private loans and remittances to foreigners.
3/ Includes no European recovery program funds since the advance of 1 billion was authorized April 3, 1948.
4/ Includes 0.8 billion for E.C.A. grants and loans utilized and 2.6 billion for all other foreign grants and loans including Army supplies for civilians in occupied areas, China aid, Greek Turkish aid, etc.
5/ Includes an estimate of the utilization during 1948 of 2.0 billion for the European recovery program and of 4.0 billion for all other U. S. Government foreign grants and loans.

4. The Government component of the gross national product, which had declined in 1946 and 1947 increased substantially during 1948. State and local Government expenditures for schools, streets and highways, as well as other Government services have been on the uptrend since the end of the war and in the first half of 1948 were at a rate about 20 percent higher than in 1947 as a whole. Federal Government expenditures are increasing substantially as a result of the expanding defense and foreign aid programs. It is estimated that federal expenditures during the year ending June 30, 1949 will be about 6 billion dollars more than in the previous fiscal year.

FOREIGN DEMAND FOR U. S. FARM PRODUCTS IN 1948

Despite the considerable improvement in the world food situation in 1948, foreign requirements of U. S. agricultural products remain large, although somewhat below the record 1947 level. As with total exports of goods and services, the value of agricultural exports in each of the first 2 quarters of 1948 was lower than in any quarter of 1947. For the second half of 1948, an increased volume of exports over the first half is indicated on the basis of large grain and cotton crops in this country and increasing utilization of ECA and other available foreign aid funds. For 1948 as a whole, the value of agricultural exports may total 3.4 billion dollars compared with 3.9 billions in 1947.

Table 5.-Value of exports in United States agricultural products in specified periods 1/

(Million dollars)

Period	Cotton including linters	Tobacco unmanu- factured 2/	Grain and prepa- rations	Other foods	Total foods 3/	Grand total 4/
	(1)	(2)	(3)	(4)	(5)	(6)
1935-39 Annual average	318	128	95	178	273	748
1947						
1st. quarter	169	93	439	317	756	1,071
2nd. quarter	137	53	511	291	802	1,038
3rd. quarter	37	52	499	280	779	919
4th. quarter	84	73	417	293	710	882
Total 1947	427	271	1,866	1,181	3,047	3,911
1948						
1st. quarter	122	40	416	236	653	859
2nd. quarter	98	41	400	208	609	785
Estimated total 1948						(3,400)

1/ In postwar period includes army supply shipments to foreign civilians in occupied area. 2/ Includes trimmings, scrap, and stems. 3/ Defined as the sum of Agricultural Crude Foodstuffs (Economic Class 2) plus Agricultural Manufactured Foodstuffs (Economic Class 4). 4/ The sum of columns 1, 2, and 5 plus small values of agricultural non-foods not shown separately.

As in the previous year (see table 5), grain shipments made up about half of the total value of agricultural exports in the first half of 1948. A considerable increase in these shipments is underway in the second half. Larger shipments of cotton and tobacco are also indicated for the remainder of the year.

DEMAND PROSPECTS FOR 1949

Demand prospects for 1949 reflect present uncertainties relating to the international situation and to future trends in those segments of the economy in which backlogs are being worked off and postwar expansion programs are being completed. Nevertheless, the growing rate of government expenditures for the national defense gives some degree of assurance for a high level of demand, at least in the first half of 1949.

The defense program is affecting the economy in the second half of this year and will be a growing force in the first half of 1949. A continued high level of exports of industrial and agricultural commodities also is assured for the first half of next year under the foreign aid programs in operation. The growing requirements for defense and foreign aid imposed on an economy already operating close to capacity pose the possibility that further inflationary pressures may develop during this period. Even if some easing occurs elsewhere in the economy, overall activity and domestic demand for farm products in the first half of 1949 are likely to be at least as high as in the last half of 1948.

Demand prospects are more uncertain for the second half of 1949 when marketings from the new crops will be heavy. They depend to a large extent on the size of future appropriations for national defense and for foreign aid. Barring any substantial reduction from 1948 in the size of these appropriations, no appreciable decline in economic activity can be foreseen. Under the programs tentatively projected earlier this year for 1949-50, some increase in appropriations for the national defense and only a slight decrease in foreign aid appropriations were indicated. New appropriations of this size, along with expected carry-overs of several billions from this year's appropriations, would provide a steadily increasing influence in the economy through the year. Furthermore, state and local governments are steadily increasing their expenditures for schools, streets, and highways. This trend is likely to continue upward through 1949. Another element of strength for next year is the continued shortage in automobiles, production of which in 1949 is likely to be limited only by the materials available to the industry. While the downward trend in recent months in new dwelling starts suggests the possibility that 1949 residential construction may be less than this year, it is likely to continue to be a strong force in the economy.

On the basis of current information, business expenditures for new plant and equipment, which have been very large in recent years, are likely to turn down in 1949. Recent unoffical surveys indicate that a substantially lower level of expenditures by manufacturing concerns is in prospect. However, expansion programs by public utilities are far from complete and should provide support in this sector. Results of an official survey will be available early in 1949 and will permit a reappraisal of these trends in capital outlays.

During 1948, a weakening demand (at the current price level) for textile products and shoes has been noted. Some reductions in price and/or production is likely in these fields, in which deferred demands have largely been met.

These divergent trends, with some weakness in the private sector being more or less offset by expanding government outlays, will tend to produce a stable overall level in 1949. Chances for price stability in 1949 appear to be stronger than in previous years, partly because another year of high production has helped reduce deferred demands. The record farm crops this year also indicate an easing in inflationary forces. If further general price advances are avoided in the near future, wage increases next spring are likely to be moderate and may not be reflected so readily in higher prices as in 1948.

To the extent that consumer incomes are maintained close to this year's level, the general level of agricultural prices in 1949 may be only slightly below 1948. For most major crops, prices have declined, or are declining, to support levels. No significant further drop in the general level can occur for the current crop. Even if crop production should again be large next year, only minor overall adjustments would be possible under the price support program scheduled to be in effect for the 1949 crops.

Lower prices for feed and some other commodities purchased by farmers next year are likely to be reflected in a minor decline in support prices. Some strength in the crop price situation also is indicated by the heavy foreign demand and the expected increase in livestock operations which will increase the outlets for feed grains. Continued heavy foreign demands are likely if the European recovery program is extended in line with the present program. While some easing in the demand for food grains is likely if further improvement occurs in European crop production, it will probably be offset by larger exports of cotton and tobacco, and of feed grains to rebuild livestock numbers.

The major possibilities for price declines are in the livestock and livestock products group. The 1948 record corn crop will be reflected in increases in supplies in the second half of 1949. Consequently, prices received by farmers for this group are likely to average somewhat lower in the second half of 1949 than in the first half.

While crop production in 1949 is likely to be somewhat smaller than this year's record, increasing livestock output will probably maintain the total volume of farm marketings at about the same level as in 1948. Cash receipts from farm marketings may be down slightly. Realized net income of farm operators is also likely to be down from 1948 levels as production costs in 1949 are likely to be about as high as this year.

This rough balance of economic forces projected for 1949 could be upset by changes in the precarious international situation. If a large increase in the defense and foreign aid program becomes necessary, inflationary forces are likely to be reinforced. On the other hand, substantial cut-backs in these programs could result in a moderate drop in activity and a weakening demand for farm products in late 1949. Under the latter conditions, prices of livestock and livestock products, as a group, would decline substantially as consumer incomes recede. Nevertheless, income from crops would be fairly well maintained by price supports and total receipts from farm marketings in 1949 would probably not be down more than 10 percent from 1948's high level.

FARM INCOME

Next year on the whole is likely to be another good year for farm incomes--but perhaps not as good as either this year or last year.

Farmers' gross income is leveling off. Their production expenses are still on the upgrade; and net income has probably passed its peak. But while farmers' realized net income may show a decline in 1949, it will probably remain higher than it was at any time before 1946.

Farmers' cash receipts from marketings in 1948 will probably total close to 30 billion dollars, or only slightly below last year. Government payments to farmers, the value of products consumed directly in farm households, and the rental value of farm dwellings have also shown little change. So farmers' total gross income in 1948 will be close to last year's level of 34.7 billion dollars.

Almost every type of farm-production expense is higher this year, however, and the total of all expenses for the year as a whole will probably be up by about 7 percent. As a result, realized net income in 1948 may drop to 16.5 billion dollars, or 8 percent below 1947.

In 1949, farmers' cash receipts and total gross income are not expected to decline very much from current levels. With production expenses likely to remain high, however, net income may slide off noticeably for the second year in a row. There is a likelihood of a decline in the prices paid by farmers for some commodities used in production. Feed prices will average lower. But with such important items as taxes, labor costs, depreciation charges, interest payments, and motor-vehicle operating costs likely to equal or exceed current levels in 1949, total production expenses will probably be about as high.

There will also be some further changes in the distribution of farm income among the various commodities and commodity groups in 1949. Total crop receipts this year will probably be about 5 percent lower than they were last year, but the total for livestock and livestock products will be up a little. A similar relationship seems likely in 1949. Receipts from many crops are expected to show some decline; but livestock and livestock products may be maintained generally near 1948 levels.

LIVESTOCK AND MEATS

Prices of meat and meat animals in 1949 are likely to continue far above war and prewar levels.

Total meat production will be little different from 1948, and the 1949 average price for all meats and meat animals is expected to be about the same as this year if industrial activity and consumer income do not decline significantly. However, seasonal changes in prices will occur, and the sharply increased hog marketings expected late in 1949 probably will cause pork and hog prices to drop more than they normally do at that time of year. Prices of beef and beef cattle are expected to remain relatively higher than prices of pork and hogs.

Even though meat output in 1949 will not be much, if any, greater than in 1948, the year may mark the turning point in the current downtrend. This is especially likely if corn and other feed crops are large next fall. In 1948, the Nation's inventory of meat animals has shrunk for the fifth consecutive year.

Meat supplies next year will again be larger than prewar but short relative to employment and incomes. Civilian consumption per person is expected to be approximately 140 to 145 pounds compared with 145 pounds in 1948, 155 in 1947 and an average of 134 pounds in 1937-41.

The 1949 meat supplies will contain more pork and less beef than in 1948. Because more of the cattle will be grain fed, however, more of the beef will be of the better grades. Supplies of meat in both mid-summer and late fall are expected to exceed those of this year. Pork production probably will increase more than usual late in the year as hogs raised from the expected large spring pig crop move to market.

Since total meat output will be little different next year, changes in prices of meats and meat animals will be due mainly to changes in demand. A continued strong consumer demand would hold 1949 prices close to those of 1948. However, the retail value of meat in 1948 has been exceptionally high in relation to incomes. If consumers' expenditures return to a pattern more like that of prewar years, meat-animal prices could weaken moderately in 1949. Even so, they would still be well above any year except 1948.

Increased pork production will result from the larger pig crops expected and from feeding to slightly heavier weights. The pig crop of this fall, which will be marketed next spring and summer, probably will be somewhat larger than the fall pig crop of 1947. With abundant corn supplies and a hog-corn ratio this fall that may be a record high, the pig crop next spring may be 15 to 20 percent larger than the 1948 spring crop. An increase of 17 percent would meet the goal of 60 million spring pigs announced by the Department of Agriculture. This would be larger than any spring pig crop since 1943.

The year 1948 is the fourth in a row when marketings of cattle and calves together with death losses exceeded additions to herds through births and imports. This increased current beef supplies at the expense of future production. The reductions have been greatest in heifers, steers, and young stock. Cows other than dairy cows have not been reduced very much. A strong demand for beef, both current and prospective, coupled with large feed supplies, is likely to result in more grain feeding of cattle this winter.

The long decline in sheep numbers, which began in 1942, is continuing. The 1948 lamb crop was down 8 percent from last year. Many ewes are again being marketed this year. Wool prices in mid-1948 showed their greatest strength since 1946, and may average well above support in 1949 because of strong demand and premium prices for the finer qualities.

The greatest single factor underlying the 1949 meat outlook is the bumper feed grain harvest of 1948. The biggest corn crop in history is the base for record feed grain supplies. The total supply of feed concentrates, although short of 1942 in tonnage, is the largest ever relative to livestock numbers.

DAIRY PRODUCTS

Prices for milk and dairy products in 1949 probably will average about the same as this year. Demand will continue near 1948 levels since consumer incomes per person are likely to be about as large as in 1948, over-all dairy exports may increase slightly, and the United States population will be slightly larger. Production of milk is likely to be slightly greater than in 1948.

The number of cows is declining for the fifth consecutive year. Farmers will have fewer cows in 1949 than in any year since the early 1930's and 12 or 13 percent fewer than at the 1944 peak. However, supplies of feed per animal unit will be a record. Dairy product-feed price relationships will be considerably more favorable to farmers than in 1948. This will result in heavier feeding and the rate of output per cow in 1949 probably will exceed this year's record of over 5,000 pounds. Total milk output will be a little greater than the expected 117 billion pounds for 1948. Favorable dairy-product feed price relationships and probably less attractive alternative opportunities in the last half of 1949 may halt the decline in milk cow numbers by the beginning of 1950.

Cash farm receipts from the sale of milk and dairy products in 1949 probably will be little different from the 4-1/2 billion dollars of this year. Declines in feed costs are likely to more than offset any increases in other items used in dairy production, so that net income from dairying probably will be at least as great, and possibly somewhat greater, than in 1948.

Production of milk on a per capita basis for 1949 will be the lowest since the drought years of the 1930's except possibly 1948. Exports will be well above prewar although still a small proportion of total production. Per capita supplies of fluid milk, and manufactured dairy products will be near 1948 levels and, except for butter, well above any prewar year.

Butter consumption this year will be about 10 pounds per person, about 40 percent below the prewar rate. This has been partly offset by increased consumption of margarine from about 3 pounds per person in prewar years to 6 pounds this year. Since the consumption of fluid milk and cream will be large in 1949, and production of milk in main butter areas will increase little if any, butter production and consumption will be low again next year.

POULTRY AND EGGS

Prices of eggs are likely to average almost as high in 1949 as in 1948. During the first two quarters, prices may be slightly higher, but in the last quarter somewhat lower, than during the same period of 1948. Support prices may approximate those in 1948. Purchases for support during the first half of 1949 may be smaller than in the same period this year since production probably will be down about 3 percent. By the fourth quarter of 1949, however egg production may be running higher than during the latter months of 1948. For the year as a whole, output is expected to be about the same as in 1948.

Farm prices for chickens, broilers, and turkeys probably will average lower in 1949 than this year, with most of the decrease during the latter months of the year. More favorable egg-feed price relationships during late 1948 and early 1949 are expected to result in a substantial increase in the number of farm chickens raised in 1949. Commercial broiler output may be about as large in total as in 1948. The 1949 turkey crop may increase substantially because of record turkey prices and lower feed prices in late 1948 and early 1949.

Domestic demand for poultry products is likely to remain strong through most of 1949. Consumer expenditures for eggs, chickens, and turkeys probably will be close to 1948 levels. Less than 4 percent of 1948 egg supplies and an insignificant percentage of poultry went to foreign outlets. Such outlets are likey to take smaller quantities in 1949.

With total supplies of eggs about the same in 1949 as in 1948 per capita consumption will be about the same. On the other hand, increased supplies of chicken and turkeys will make possible moderate increases in per capita consumption of those items.

FATS, OILS, AND OILSEEDS

The general level of fat-and-oil prices is likely to be moderately lower in the year beginning October 1948 than last year, largely as a result of increased domestic production of fats and oils. In 1947-48, the index of wholesale prices of 27 major fats and oils averaged 274 (1935-39=100), a new peak, compared with 263 in 1946-47 and about 150 during most of the war.

Total output of fats and oils from domestic materials in the year beginning October 1948 may be 3 to 4 percent larger than the output of 9.9 billion pounds in 1947-48. Bumper 1948 crops of oilseeds assure a material increase in production of vegetable oils in 1948-49. However, smaller stocks of edible vegetable oils this fall than last will partly offset the increase.

Output of animal fats may decline slightly in 1948-49. The 1948 spring pig crop was 3 percent smaller than a year earlier, and the number of cattle on farms January 1, 1949 is expected to be less than at the beginning of 1948. These factors probably will be partly offset by feeding of hogs and cattle to heavier weights than in 1947-48, since the supply of feeds per animal unit in 1948-49 will be at a new high.

Imports of copra into the United States in 1949 probably will be larger than in 1948, when they were reduced as a result of typhoon damage to Philippine coconut groves in December 1947. Imports of palm oil also may increase, since exports from the Netherlands Indies, the leading prewar source for the United States, are expected to expand in 1949. European demand for fats and oils from the United States remains strong.

Disappearance of fats and oils in the year beginning October 1948 is likely to increase, reflecting the rise in production. A moderate increase is probable in consumption of food fats and in use of oils in drying-oil products. Use of fats in soap may remain about the same as in 1947-48.

Disappearance of fats and oils in the year ended June 1948, the latest 12-month period for which data are available, totaled about 70 pounds per person (fat content), the same as prewar. Disappearance of food fats, at about 43 pounds per person (fat content) was 3 pounds under the 1937-41 average, but use of fats in nonfood products was about 27 pounds per person, 3 pounds above prewar.

Prices to growers for soybeans produced in 1948 are to be supported at $2.18 per bushel, 14 cents per bushel above the support for the 1947 crop but more than $1.00 below the season average price. Prices to farmers for soybeans were near the support when the marketing season began in late September but probably will rise later. The longer term outlook for soybeans remains favorable. Much research work is being done to improve soybean oil for both edible and drying oil uses. And a large potential export market for soybeans will exist as long as only small quantities of Manchurian soybeans are available to Western Europe.

The price of flaxseed produced in 1948 is being supported at $6.00 per bushel, Minneapolis basis, the same level as for the 1947 crop. The large crop of 47.3 million bushels this year together with the carryin of 7.3 million bushels, is at least 14 million bushels larger than the probable quantity needed to supply domestic uses and to provide for a normal carryout. Export allocations of 2 million bushels of flaxseed were announced in September, largely to countries of Western Europe and to the Department of the Army. Additional allocations of oilseeds, including flaxseed, are under consideratio

The record 1948 peanut crop of 2.3 billion pounds, picked and threshed, is approximately 1.0 billion pounds larger than the quantity that will be used commercially in edible products, used and lost on farms, and sold by farmers for local consumption. Part of the excess 1.0 billion pounds will be crushed in the United States, and part will be exported, largely for crushing abroad. In 1947-48, when the peanut crop was somewhat less than that expected for 1948-49, about 0.4 billion pounds were crushed in the United States and 0.5 billion pounds were exported.

Commercial use of peanuts in edible products has declined substantially since the war. During the war, peanuts and peanut butter were substituted for scarce foods, particularly candy and jam, which have become relatively abundant again. In addition, the price of peanuts to growers has been maintained at 90 percent of the parity price at the beginning of the marketing season. Ninety percent of the parity price July 15, 1948 was 10.8 cents per pound compared with 10.0 cents a year earlier.

CORN AND OTHER FEED

Chiefly as a result of the marked increase in production of corn, and other feed grains, feed prices are expected to average much lower in 1948-49 than in the past feeding season. Prices of nearly all feeds have declined in recent months. Prices of oats, barley, and grain sorghums reached Government support levels in August. Corn prices have been high in relation to most other grains this past summer, but have declined sharply in recent weeks. The seasonal decline will be much greater. Prices of all feed grains are expected to be close to the Government support levels this fall and winter and to be unusually low in relation to livestock prices.

Feed supply prospects for the 1947-48 feeding season are about the best in history. The total feed concentrate supply will be about 166 million tons, more than one-fifth larger than in 1948-48 and only a little smaller than the record supply of 1942-43 when wheat feedings were the second largest of record. The total feed supply will be the largest on record in relation to the number of livestock to be fed.

The total production of feed grains will be 8 percent above the previous record in 1946. Even with a small carry-over this year, the total feed grain supply also is larger than in any other year. The very large production of feed grains in the Midwest will result in large sales by farmers, particularly of corn, during the coming year. This will substantially increase the quantity available to deficit feed areas, for domestic food and industrial uses, and for exports. Even after allowing for liberal use of feed grains during the coming year, the carry-over of feed grains at the end of 1948-49 is expected to be the largest in recent years - probably around the high 1937-41 average.

Exports of the 4 feed grains, probably will total close to the 5 million tons of 1946-47, much larger than the export of about 1.7 million tons in 1947-48. Much of the increase from 1947-48 will be in corn.

Near record supplies of byproduct feeds will again be available for live-stock feeding this year - probably close to the 19 million tons fed in 1947-48. Total high protein feed supplies are expected to be a little larger than last year's near record in relation to the number of livestock to be fed.

With large supplies of other feeds, less wheat is expected to be fed during the 1948-49 feeding year, probably the smallest amount since 1940-41.

The total hay supply for this year is the smallest since 1941, but it is near record in relation to the reduced number of livestock on farms. The hay-supply situation varies widely by regions. Although supplies are ample in most sections of the country, in some areas, especially in the dairy region of the Midwest, and some of the range states hay supplies will be short this season.

WHEAT

With United States wheat supplies again very large and disappearance expected to be smaller in 1948-49, stocks next July 1 will increase for the second straight year. The supply of wheat in the United States in 1948-49 will provide about 730 million bushels for export and carry-over. The crop is being moved rapidly into export but the total for the year hardly seems likely to amount to as much as last year. During the 1948-49 marketing year, the carry-over is likely to be increased from 195 million bushels on hand at the beginning of the season to around 275 million on July 1, 1949.

Farmers seeded 77.7 million acres of winter and spring wheat for the 1948 crop in spite of unfavorable drought conditions in the Southwest at seeding time. If farmers seeded this acreage for the 1949 crop and average yields were obtained, a crop of 1,165 million bushels would be produced. With domestic disappearance estimated at about 750 million bushels, 690 million bushels would be available for export and carry-over. If recovery abroad continues, it is expected that exports will be between 300 and 350 million bushels, which is substantially below 1948-49. Exports of this size would lead to a further increase in stocks.

Under these conditions, prices in 1949-50 again would be depressed to below loan levels in the heavy marketing season, and would average lower relative to the loan than they will in 1948-49. Furthermore, the loan level next year at 90 percent of parity is likely to be less than this year, which was $2.00 at the national farm level. Lower prices for feed grains, feedstuffs and other goods purchased by farmers may reduce the parity index sufficiently to bring the loan level down slightly.

FRUIT

Consumer demand for fruit in 1949 probably will be about the same as in 1948. However, if production in 1949 is larger than this year's below average crop, prices will be somewhat lower.

Export demand for fruit in 1949 is uncertain. Shortage of dollar exchange and import policies of both Western and Eastern Hemisphere countries continue to limit fruit exports from the United States. Imports of bananas into the United States may increase further in 1949, moderately surpassing prewar volume. Shipments of canned pineapple from Hawaii are expected to be about as large next year as in 1948.

Prices that growers will receive for the large 1948-49 citrus crop are expected to average near those for the 1947-48 crop. Production of citrus fruit in 1949-50 is expected to continue large and prices probably will be about as low as in 1947-48.

New-crop grapefruit from Florida started to market in volume in early September, the season beginning a few weeks earlier than that for the 1947-48 crop. By late September, movement of new-crop oranges was getting under way.

Production of deciduous fruit in 1949 is likely to be moderately larger than in 1948. This larger production would result in prices somewhat lower than in 1948. This year, production of the major deciduous fruits is about 9 percent smaller than in 1947.

Mainly because of smaller crops, prices that growers will receive for the 1948 crops of peaches, apples, and pears are expected to average higher than those for the 1947 crops. Prices for grapes and dried prunes may average a little higher than in 1947. But prices for cranberries probably will average lower than in 1947, partly because of larger production.

Total production of tree nuts in 1948 sets a new record, 17 percent larger than production in 1947. Partly because of increased output, prices are likely to average lower than in 1947.

The 1948 pack of frozen fruits probably will be slightly to moderately larger than the 1947 pack, with increases in strawberries and fruit juices more than offsetting any decreases in some other items. The 1948 packs of dried and canned fruits are expected to be smaller than the 1947 packs. A record pack of citrus juices was canned in the 1947-48 season and another large pack seems likely in the season ahead.

The Government has announced a program through which it will purchase up to about 200,000 tons of the 1948-49 pack of dried fruit. Such purchases will be used to assist in relief feeding in foreign countries and for school lunch and institutional feeding in this country. About 275,000 tons of the 1947-48 pack were similarly purchased and distributed.

COMMERCIAL TRUCK CROPS

For Fresh Market

Demand for fresh market truck crops through most of 1949 is expected to be about as strong as in 1948. Prices received by farmers, however, probably will average slightly lower in most months of 1949 than in the same months of 1948, because production of most of these crops probably will be somewhat larger than in 1948.

Although demand for fresh vegetables will continue strong this fall, the prices growers will receive are expected to average moderately lower than in the same months of 1947 because of larger production. Early reports on commercial crops for fall marketing indicate an output more than 20 percent larger than last fall and more than 10 percent larger than the 1937-46 average. Crop prospects are below last fall only for green lima beans and lettuce, but even these are about a third above average. Compared with last fall, crop prospects are relatively brightest for snap beans, cabbage, carrots, cucumbers, and green peas.

For Processing

Consumer demand for commercially canned and frozen vegetables is expected to continue strong this fall and throughout most of 1949.

Combined stocks of canned snap beans, sweet corn, green peas, tomatoes, and tomato juice held by canners and wholesale distributors July 1, 1948 were slightly smaller than a year earlier. Cold-storage holdings of frozen vegetables on September 1, 1948 were much smaller than a year earlier. Commercial canners and freezers of vegetables have scaled their 1948 packing operations in line with their stocks position and the rate at which their stocks have been moving into consumption. Consequently, packers will go into the 1949 season with only normal working stocks.

POTATOES AND SWEETPOTATOES

Consumer demand for 1949 crop potatoes is expected to be about as strong as it has been for the 1948 crop. However, prices which farmers will receive for potatoes probably will be substantially lower. This forecast is based on the assumption that support prices for 1949-crop potatoes will be set lower than the 90 percent of parity which applies to the 1948 crop. Under Title I of the Agricultural Act of 1948, the minimum level for price support of potatoes is reduced from 90 to 60 percent of parity.

Just what effect the prospect of lower prices may have upon farmers' intentions to plant is unknown. Acreage may not drop substantially until after lower prices have been experienced. Even then, much will depend upon what alternatives farmers may have.

The large 1948 potato crop has required price-support activity on a considerable scale. Many of the potatoes bought for price-support this year are being converted into potato flour. This outlet makes it possible to save most of the food value of the potatoes and converts a perishable product to one which can be stored successfully for a much longer time.

Demand for sweetpotatoes in most of 1949 is expected to be fully as strong as in 1948.

The small 1948 crop of sweetpotatoes probably will command slightly higher prices on the average than those for the 1947 crop. However, prices may drop to support levels temporarily if farmers attempt to move their crop to market too fast at digging time.

DRY EDIBLE BEANS AND PEAS

Demand for dry edible beans in 1949 probably will be moderately lower than in 1948, mainly because of an expected reduction in export demand. During the war and early postwar years, beans moved readily into foreign outlets to supplement foreign production of beans and other foods. With foreign production increased considerably above the low levels at the end of the war, however, foreign demand for beans from the United States probably will be considerably lower in 1949 than in 1948. Consumer demand for beans in the United States probably will be about the same in 1949 as in 1948. But with lower total demand, grower prices are likely to be somewhat lower for beans in 1949 than in 1948.

Prices received by growers for 1948-crop beans may average as much as 25 percent lower than the average of $12.10 per 100 pounds for the 1947 crop. Prices for 1947-crop beans were generally above support levels. But with the approach of the 1948-49 marketing season, prices declined, and in mid-September some varieties of new-crop beans were selling below supports. Support prices for the 1948 crop range from $7.70 to $9.95 per 100 pounds for U. S. No. 1 beans, cleaned and bagged, f.o.b. country shipping point. These prices reflect 90 percent of parity as of August 15, 1948, and because of an increase in parity are about 6 percent higher than supports for the 1947 crop. The 1948 crop is estimated at 19.4 million bags, 13 percent larger than the 1947 crop and 16 percent larger than the 1937-46 average. About 3 million bags of the new crop will be available for export.

Demand for dry peas in 1949 probably will be about the same as the reduced demand of 1948. Foreign outlets are not expected to take more than in 1948, when considerably less were taken than during the war and early postwar years. Grower prices are likely to be moderately lower than those for the 1948 crop.

About 3.5 million bags were produced in 1948, which is 46 percent less than in 1947 and 33 percent less than the 1937-46 average. Relatively small quantities will be available for export. Grower prices in mid-September were slightly above support, and prices for the entire crop probably will average near the $5.61 per 100 pounds for the 1947 crop.

COTTON

Domestic mill consumption dropped from a peacetime record of 10 million bales in the 1946-47 season to 9.3 million bales during the past season. The outlook for the current season is that consumption will probably be under last season. Exports of cotton textiles are expected to be smaller. Deferred demands for textiles, resulting from the war should be considerably less intense because of restocking of wardrobes and inventories from the past 2 seasons' production of fabrics. These factors, with increased rayon production, should cause smaller domestic cotton consumption.

Exports of raw cotton are expected to increase considerably above last season's 2.0 million bales, the lowest since the Civil War. The ECA program together with low stocks of raw cotton in importing foreign countries and continued restoration of textile mills, are favorable factors for increased exports. Also, the ratio of prices of American cotton to competitive foreign cotton is more favorable for exports than for the past several seasons. The increase in exports should offset the decrease in domestic mill consumption so that total disappearance will be as large as or larger than for the past season.

Because of the large 1948 domestic crop of 15.2 million bales and a 1/2 million bale increase in the carry-over, the total supply of cotton in the United States will exceed last season's by 25 percent. The carry-over at the end of the current season should be around 5 or 6 million bales, or almost double the carry-over at the beginning of the season.

The average 10 spot market prices of 15/16" Middling cotton, which averaged above 37 cents in the April-June period, declined to 31.03 cents on September 1. The average price on September 15 was 31.38 cents. The average farm price in mid-September was 30.94 cents. Prices of cotton at the farm level for various grades and staples are near or slightly below the loan level. Considerable quantities of the 1948 cotton crop will be placed under the loan program by farmers.

Domestic mill consumption in August, totaled 728,732 bales, compared with 627,393 bales in July, the lowest since July 1940, and 712,864 bales for August 1947. Cotton textile exports at the end of July had declined 1/3 below exports at the same time last year. Exports of raw cotton for the month of July were 149,000 bales, compared with 84,000 bales in July of the previous season.

WOOL

World demand for wool is expected to continue strong during the 1948-49 season. World consumption during this period probably will be near the 1947-48 level and is expected to exceed world production, which is currently estimated at 3.8 billion pounds. As a result, a further reduction in world stocks probably will take place. The high level of world consumption of choice fine wools already has resulted in a marked decline in stocks of such wools.

Domestic demand for wool textiles is expected to conform closely with the trend of industrial production and personal income. If demand remains strong, mill consumption of apparel wool during 1949 may be 850-950 million pounds, grease basis. This would be a reduction of from 5 to 15 percent from present estimates for 1948. Increased military requirements will tend to offset an expected decline in civilian demand.

Under the provisions of the Agricultural Act of 1948, the price of wool during 1949 will be supported at the 1946 price support level, approximately 42.3 cents per pound. However, as prices in foreign markets for fine staple wools are expected to remain at or near their present high levels, growers of such wools probably will be able to obtain higher prices through direct sale to mills and dealers than through the price support programs.

Imports of apparel wool probably will increase slightly during 1949. Due to the higher replacement costs of foreign wools, United States stocks are being absorbed rapidly. Indications are that domestic production in 1949 may be slightly less than in 1948. Consequently, if mill consumption is maintained at the level anticipated for 1949, manufacturers probably will have to rely more heavily on foreign wools.

TOBACCO

Consumer demand for cigarettes during 1949 is expected to continue high. Some increase may be made in use of smoking tobacco, but chewing toacco consumption will probably be slightly lower in line with the long-time trend. Consumer demand for cigars and snuff in 1949 will probably equal or slightly exceed 1948. Because of Economic Cooperation Administration operations and the progress towards economic recovery in Europe, export demand for unmanufactured tobacco in 1949 may be stronger than in 1948. Cigarette-type tobacco in 1949 will be in stronger demand than other kinds, both domestically and abroad, because of the steadily increasing use of cigarettes.

More than three-fifths of the 1948 flue-cured crop has been marketed at prices substantially higher than last year and averaging well above the support level. The strong demand for flue-cured has stemmed mainly from the record production of cigarettes, which is expected to continue at a high level during the year ahead. It is probable that the total manufacture of cigarettes this year will be near 385 billion compared with 370 billion in 1947. Domestic consumption has accounted for a great part of cigarette production, while exports, which account for 6 percent, have been running slightly above last year. Unmanufactured flue-cured is the principal export tobacco and during fiscal 1947-48, fell 35 percent from the record of 1946-47. Exports of flue-cured during 1948-49 are expected to be larger as the European Recovery Program gains headway. The 1949 flue-cured quota announcement in late August indicated that acreage allotments will be about 5 percent larger than in 1948. The Secretary of Agriculture has the authority to increase the present announced quota up to 20 percent as late as March 1, 1949, if conditions should warrant any increase.

A firm demand is expected for the Burley crop, which will go to auctions in late November or early December. The Burley loan rate is 5 percent higher than last year because of the increase in prices paid by farmers over the past 12 months. Next to flue-cured, Burley contributes the greatest volume of tobacco used in cigarettes. The high cigarette production will be a strong factor in maintaining a large disappearance of Burley during 1948-49. Exports in 1947-48 are estimated at about one-fourth less than 1946-47 but still triple prewar. Considerable quantities of Burley are also used in smoking and chewing toacco. It is estimated that production of smoking tobacco in

1948 may reach 109 million pounds, about 4 million pounds above 1947. In 1949, smoking toacco production is expected to show a small increase. The manufacture of chewing tobacco during 1948 may fall slightly below the 98-1/2 million pounds produced last year. No substantial change in chewing tobacco production is expected in 1949.

Maryland tobacco finds its greatest outlet in cigarettes and so may be expected to benefit from their continued high consumption. The auction season for the 1947 Maryland crop closed August 20. Prices averaged 41.6 cents --7 cents less than in the previous season.

Domestic use of fire-cured is largely in snuff, which for 1948 is estimated at 41 million pounds, about 5 percent larger than 1947. Snuff consumption in 1949 is expected to be about the same as or a little higher than 1948. The dark air-cured types are also used in chewing tobacco. Fire-cured and dark air-cured exports have been declining over the long term. The support levels for fire-cured and dark air-cured are 5 percent higher than last year because they are linked to the Burley loan rate. These latter types are expected to bring prices close to the support level when they go to market late this year and in the early months of 1949.

The demand for most cigar tobacco is expected to be fairly strong. Production of domestic filler tobacco is near last year while binder is moderately lower. The level of price support for cigar types has also advanced in the past year due to the increase in parity prices. The average price received from most cigar types during the 1947 marketing year exceeded the support level by a substantial margin. Cigar consumption in 1948 is estimated at around 5-3/4 million -almost 2 percent higher than 1947. Cigar consumption in 1949 is expected to equal or slightly exceed that of 1948.

Total unmanufactured tobacco exports in 1948 are expected to be around 450 million pounds (declared weight) compared with 506 million last year. Through September 30, ECA authorizations for tobacco totaled approximately 33.3 million dollars for about 79 million pounds.

SUGAR

Supplies of and demand for sugar have returned to prewar levels. Prices of sugar are lower this year than last. It is estimated that sugar consumption will be about 95 to 100 pounds per person for 1948, compared with about 90 pounds in 1947 and an average of about 96 pounds in 1935-39.

Production of sugar in the 1947 48 crop year in areas normally supplying the United States was the largest on record. While production in 1948-49 is expected to be somewhat less, largely because of an anticipated reduction in the Cuban crop of one million tons from this year's record output, supplies will be over 25 percent larger than the 1935-39 average. Also the demand of other foreign countries for Cuban sugar may be reduced because of anticipated increases in production in importing countries.

U. S. Department of Agriculture
Washington 25, D. C.

OFFICIAL BUSINESS

DPS-10/48-6200
PERMIT NO. 1001

Penalty for private use to avoid
payment of postage $300

FOREST PRODUCTS

Demand for forest products in 1949 is expected to continue generally strong and prices to remain high, although some decline from the 1948 level is likely. A continued high level of construction activity, both for housing and non-residential purposes, should sustain the major demands for lumber, and indirectly for sawlogs and stumpage. Requirements for shipping containers and for factory products likewise should remain at high levels on the basis of expected business activity and employment. During the past 3 years approxi mately 6 billion board feet have been added to lumber stocks at mills and yard bringing total stocks on hand to about 60 percent of the prewar level. How- ever, dealers are unlikely to continue increasing lumber stocks in the face of current high price levels, and this factor may be expected to result in an easing of the total demand for lumber.

Domestic production of lumber in 1948 is estimated at approximately 38 billion board feet. With estimated imports of 1.8 billion feet, exports of nearly 0.9 billion feet, and an allowance for additions to stocks, 1948 domestic consumption is estimated at 37.5 billion board feet, the highest level since 1943. There is little likelihood that expected decreases in domestic demands in 1949 will be offset by expanded exports in view of dollar shortages in foreign countries.

A reduction in demand for lumber in 1949 probably will lead to some decline in prices, particularly for the poorer common grades. Markets for low quality stumpage, small timber, and less preferred species will be af- fected most adversely. Production of lumber in 1949 may be somewhat lower than in 1948, both as a result of an easing in prices and the continued existence of such factors as limited supply and high cost of available stumpage and high production costs.

Demand for pulpwood is expected to remain strong and prices high in 1949 with little or no change from the high levels of 1948. Continued strong markets for veneer logs, used in the manufacture of shipping containers and plywood, and for minor products such as poles and piling, may also be expecte

Lightning Source UK Ltd.
Milton Keynes UK
UKHW010606120219
337137UK00007B/1573/P